Houghton
Mifflin
Harcourt

D1594932

Language Arts

Grade 1

Printed in the U.S.A.

ISBN 978-0-544-26784-8

3 4 5 6 7 8 9 10   0928   22 21 20 19 18 17 16 15

4500539968   A B C D E F G

Core Skills Language Arts
GRADE 1
Table of Contents

* Aligns to the English Language Arts Common Core State
  Standards for grade 1.

Table of Contents
Core Skills Language Arts, Grade 1

Introduction

Core Skills Language Arts was developed to help your child improve the language skills he or she needs to succeed. The book emphasizes skills in the key areas of

- grammar,
- punctuation,
- vocabulary,
- writing, and
- research.

The lessons included in the book provide many opportunities for your child to practice and apply important language and writing skills. These skills will help your child excel in all academic areas, increase his or her scores on standardized tests, and have a greater opportunity for success in his or her career.

About the Book

The book is divided into six units:

- Parts of Speech
- Sentences
- Mechanics
- Vocabulary and Usage
- Writing
- Research Skills

Your child can work through each unit of the book, or you can pinpoint areas for extra practice. Many pages contain information boxes about the concept presented on the page. The best approach would be to read this information to the child and then let the child complete the exercises on the page.

Lessons have specific instructions and examples and arc designed for your child to complete independently. Grammar lessons range from using nouns and verbs to writing better sentences. Writing exercises range from the personal story to the book report. With this practice, your child will gain extra confidence as he or she works on daily school lessons or standardized tests.

A thorough answer key is also provided to check the quality of answers.

A Step Toward Success

Practice may not always make perfect, but it is certainly a step in the right direction. The activities in *Core Skills Language Arts* are an excellent way to ensure greater success for your child.

Unit 1: Parts of Speech
Naming Words

Naming words are called **nouns**.
Nouns name people, places, and things.
Examples: man   house   boat

Look at each picture. Say the naming word for each picture. Then, write the naming word on the line. Color the pictures.

1. boy

people

3. dog

animals

2. girl

people

4. cat

animals

Name ___Anya Bajaj___ S   Date ___8-79-17___

Naming Words for People

Some nouns name people.
Examples: sister   teacher   dad

Read the words in the box. Look at each picture. Name the people. Write words from the box.

| farmer   doctor   cook   worker |

1.

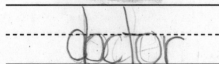
doctor

3.

worker

2.

farmer

4.

cook

Unit 1
Core Skills Language Arts, Grade 1

Name _Anya Bajaj_   Date _8-19-r_

Naming Words for Animals

Some nouns name animals.
Examples:
pig   horse   whale

Complete each sentence. Write a word from the box.

frog	fish	dog	cat	bird	fox

1. A _fish_ swims in the sea.

2. A _frog_ jumps out of a pond.

3. A _fox_ runs in the woods.

4. A _bird_ flies in the sky.

5. A _dog_ barks.

6. A _cat_ meows.

Unit 1
Core Skills Language Arts, Grade 1

Name Anya Bajaj   Date 8-19-17

Naming Words for Places

Some nouns name places.
Examples: city   beach   library

Read the words in the box. Look at each picture. Name the place. Write a word from the box.

| house   farm   lake   park |

1.

lake

3.

park

2.

house

4.

farm

Unit 1
Core Skills Language Arts, Grade 1

Naming Words for Things

> Some nouns name things.
> *Examples:* toy   chair   shoes

Complete each sentence. Write a word from the box.

cup	hat	bed	apple	crayons	box

1. I drink milk from a _____.

2. I use _____ for coloring.

3. I eat an _____ for lunch.

4. I sleep in a _____.

5. I wear a _____ on my head.

6. I keep my toys in a _____.

Unit 1
Core Skills Language Arts, Grade 1

Two Kinds of Naming Words

Some words name common things. These words are called **common nouns**.

Examples: child   park   story

Some words name special things. These words are called **proper nouns**. They begin with capital letters.

Examples:

S̲am   P̲eace P̲ark   "T̲he R̲ed P̲ony"

Read each sentence. Circle the special name in each sentence. Then, write the special name on the line.

1. That boy is Chris. _____

2. That girl is Lina. _____

3. My friend is Lee Chin. _____

4. I live on Main Street. _____

5. I read "All About Worms." _____

Unit 1
Core Skills Language Arts, Grade 1

Naming Words That Show Ownership

Some nouns show who owns or has something. These nouns end with **'s**.

Examples: Mark has a pen.   It is <u>Mark's</u> pen.

The cat has a toy.   It is the <u>cat's</u> toy.

Ana owns a car.   It is <u>Ana's</u> car.

Complete each sentence. Write a naming word from the box.

doll's	Dad's	teacher's	dog's

1. It is the _____ stick.

2. The _____ desk is big.

3. _____ hammer is heavy.

4. My _____ hair is long.

Naming One and More Than One

A naming word can name **one**.

A naming word can name **more than one**.

Many naming words add <u>s</u> to name more than one.

Example: one **cat**

two **cats**

Write the naming word in ( ) to complete each sentence.

1. I see two _____.
(bird, birds)

2. I see one _____.
(bug, bugs)

3. I see two _____.
(girl, girls)

4. I see one _____.
(dog, dogs)

5. I see three _____.
(frog, frogs)

I and Me

The words I and me take the place of some naming words.

Use I in the naming part of a sentence.
The word I is always written as a capital letter.

Use me in the telling part of a sentence.
Examples: **I** have a new dog.
The dog licks **me**.

Write I or me to complete each sentence.

1. _____ am a big red hen.

2. Can you find _____?

3. _____ am not in the henhouse.

4. Surprise! _____ am in the garden!

5. Now you can see _____.

We and They

The words <u>we</u> and <u>they</u> take the place of some naming words.

Use <u>we</u> and <u>they</u> in the naming part of a sentence.
Examples: <u>Jim and I</u> will talk.
We will talk.

<u>Kay and Chris</u> will talk.
They will talk.

Rewrite each sentence. Write <u>We</u> or <u>They</u> to take the place of the underlined names.

1. <u>Sam and I</u> are here.

   _____
   -
   _____

2. <u>Kay and Amy</u> are not here.

   _____
   -
   _____

3. <u>Kim and I</u> will play ball.

   _____
   -
   _____

4. <u>Ann, Pat, and Chad</u> found a kitten.

   _____
   -
   _____

Name _____ Date _____

He, She, and It

The words <u>he</u>, <u>she</u>, and <u>it</u> take the place of some naming words.

Use <u>he</u> for a man or a boy.

Use <u>she</u> for a woman or a girl.

Use <u>it</u> for an animal or a thing.

Examples: **He** rows the boat.

She rides in **it**.

Rewrite each sentence. Use <u>He</u>, <u>She</u>, or <u>It</u> in place of the underlined words.

1. <u>Amy</u> likes to write.

_____

- -

_____

2. <u>John</u> likes to read.

_____

- -

_____

3. The <u>book</u> is on the table.

_____

- -

_____

4. <u>Jenna</u> saw the bird.

_____

- -

_____

My, Their, His, Her, and Its

The words <u>my</u>, <u>their</u>, <u>his</u>, <u>her</u>, and <u>its</u> take the place of some naming words. These words show that something belongs to a person or thing.

Use <u>my</u> for something that belongs to you.

Use <u>their</u> for something that belongs to two or more people.

Use <u>his</u> for something that belongs to a man or boy.

Use <u>her</u> for something that belongs to a woman or girl.

Use <u>its</u> for something that belongs to an animal or thing.

Examples: I tied <u>my</u> shoes.

The boy won <u>his</u> race.

Rewrite each sentence. Use <u>my</u>, <u>their</u>, <u>his</u>, <u>her</u>, or <u>its</u> in place of the underlined words.

1. Mom and Dad wash <u>Mom and Dad's</u> car.

_____

- -

_____

2. The boy plays with <u>the boy's</u> car.

_____

- -

_____

3. I play with <u>the girl's</u> puppy.

_____

- -

_____

Nobody, Anyone, Everybody, Nothing, Anything, and Everything

> The words nobody, anyone, everybody, nothing, anything, and everything can tell about an unknown person or thing.
>
> Use words with every to mean all (everybody, everything).
>
> Use words with no to mean none (nobody, nothing).
>
> Use words with any to mean any (anyone, anything).
>
> *Examples:*   Everybody sat at the table.
> Is anything in the basket?
> There is nothing in the basket.

Write Nobody, Anyone, Everybody, Nothing, Anything, or Everything to complete each sentence.

1. _____ is in the room.

2. _____ went on a trip.

3. We cleaned the room. _____

   is on our desks.

4. _____ was put away.

Action Words

An **action word** tells what someone or something does. Action words are called **verbs**.

Examples: Tom **sleeps**.
Birds **fly**.
Dogs **bark**.

Complete each sentence. Write an action word from the box.

| talks | ride | eats | sing | waves |

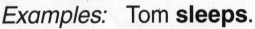

1. The girl _____ the food.

2. Dad _____ good-bye.

3. The boy _____ on the phone.

4. We _____ songs.

5. We _____ our bikes.

Using Clear Action Words

Some action words tell exactly how people and things move.

Examples: The dog **moves** across the grass.

The dog **races** across the grass.

Complete each sentence. Write the word in ( ) that tells exactly how each animal moves.

1. The fish _____ in the lake.
   (swims, stays)

2. The rabbit _____ up and down.
   (goes, hops)

3. The snake _____ on the ground.
   (sits, crawls)

4. The birds _____ in the sky.
   (fly, move)

Unit 1
Core Skills Language Arts, Grade 1

Action Words with One or More Than One

Action words can tell what one person or thing does. Action words can also tell what more than one person or thing does.

Add <u>s</u> to an action word that tells about one person or thing.

Example: The two boys **play** ball.

The one boy **plays** ball.

Complete each sentence. Write an action word.

1. The two girls _____ rope.

The one girl _____ rope.

2. The balls _____ slowly.

The ball _____ slowly.

3. The dogs _____.

The dog _____.

Unit 1
Core Skills Language Arts, Grade 1

Action Words About Now

> An action word can tell about now. Action words that tell about one end with s̲. Action words that tell about more than one do not end with s̲.
>
> *Examples:* Ray **helps** his dad.
>
> Sam and Sara **throw** the ball.

Circle the action word in each sentence.

1. The sun shines all day long.

2. The seeds grow in the garden.

3. The frog hops on the log.

Complete each sentence. Choose the correct action word in ( ). Write the word on the line.

4. The flowers _____ water.
(need, needs)

5. The boy _____ some water.
(get, gets)

Name _____ Date _____

Action Words About the Past

An action word can tell about the past. Some action words that tell about the past end with ed.

Examples: A mother duck **walked** across the grass.

She **quacked** for the little ducks.

Complete each sentence. Write the word in ( ) that tells about the past.

1. Two little ducks _____ in the water.
   (plays, played)

2. The mother duck _____ at them.
   (look, looked)

3. Two little ducks _____ out of the water.
   (jumped, jump)

4. They all _____ away.
   (walk, walked)

Action Words About Later

An action word can tell about something that is going to happen later. To tell about the future, use <u>will</u> with the action word.

Examples: Tonight I <u>will watch</u> TV.
Then I <u>will brush</u> my teeth.
Tomorrow I <u>will wake</u> up early.

Complete each sentence. Write the word or words in ( ) that tell about later.

1. Tomorrow I (have, will have) a party.

_____

- -

_____

2. My friends (will come, come).

_____

- -

_____

3. We (eat, will eat) cake.

_____

- -

_____

4. We (played, will play) games.

_____

- -

_____

Unit 1
Core Skills Language Arts, Grade 1

Using Is and Are

Use is to tell about one person or thing now.

Use are to tell about more than one person or thing now.

Examples: Jack **is** sick today.

Jack's friends **are** sick, too.

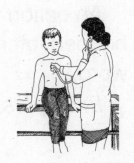

Complete each sentence. Write is or are.

1. He _____ my father.

2. She _____ my mother.

3. They _____ in the garden.

4. Sue and I _____ in the garden, too.

5. The flowers _____ pretty.

6. Our dog _____ black and white.

Using <u>Was</u> and <u>Were</u>

Use <u>was</u> to tell about one person or thing in the past.

Use <u>were</u> to tell about more than one person or thing in the past.

Examples: One cat **was** on the mat.

Two cats **were** on the bench.

Complete each sentence. Write <u>was</u> or <u>were</u>.

1. I _____ at the lake.

2. Carl and Bert _____ there, too.

3. We _____ going to sleep.

4. The rain _____ a big surprise.

5. The tent _____ all wet.

6. Dad _____ calling us.

Using See, Come, and Run

Use see, come, and run to tell about something that happens now.

Use saw, came, and ran to tell about something that happened in the past.

Examples: I **see** a red balloon now.

Dad **came** home yesterday.

Complete each sentence. Circle the correct action word in ( ).

1. Last night Kim (run, ran) to the store.

2. Now I (run, ran) to the store.

3. Last week Bob (see, saw) a new movie.

4. Yesterday Tina (come, came) to my house.

5. Now Tina and Kim (come, came) to my house.

Write sentences. Use the word in ( ) in your sentence.

6. (see)

_____

- -

_____

7. (run)

_____

- -

_____

Using <u>Go</u> and <u>Went</u>

The words <u>go</u> and <u>went</u> are action words.
Use <u>go</u> to tell about now. Use <u>went</u> to tell
about the past.

Examples: ·Today we **go** to school.

Last week we **went** to the beach.

Write <u>go</u> or <u>went</u> to complete each sentence.

1. Last Friday we _____ to the park.

2. Yesterday we _____ swimming.

3. Now we _____ home.

4. Last night my cat _____ outside.

5. Now I _____ outside.

6. My cat and I _____ inside now.

Contractions with <u>Not</u>

A **contraction** is a word made by joining two words. An **apostrophe (')** shows where a letter or letters are left out. Many contractions are made with the word <u>not</u>.

Examples: do + not = **don't**
              had + not = **hadn't**
              will + not = **won't**

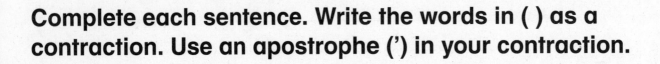

Complete each sentence. Write the words in ( ) as a contraction. Use an apostrophe (') in your contraction.

1. I _____ like snakes.
   (do not)

2. I _____ go near a snake.
   (will not)

3. You _____ make me touch one.
   (can not)

4. Zack _____ here.
   (is not)

5. I _____ seen him all day.
   (have not)

Words That Tell Where and When

Some words describe action words. They tell when or where an action happens.

Examples: Do you like to play <u>outside</u>?
I played at the park <u>yesterday</u>.
<u>Tomorrow</u> I will fly a kite.
The kite will fly <u>high</u>.
<u>Now</u> I am hungry.

**Complete each sentence. Choose a word from the box.
Write it on the line.**

outside	inside	today	Soon	always

1. I played with my dog Fifi _____ .

2. We went _____ to play.

3. Fifi _____ catches the ball.

4. _____ Fifi was tired.

5. She wanted to go _____ to nap.

Unit 1
Core Skills Language Arts, Grade 1

Describing Words

Describing words tell about naming words.

Examples: **three** birds
              tall boy
              little bear
              happy girl

Circle each describing word. Then, write it on the line.

1. green frog

_____

- - - - - - - - - - - - - - - -

_____

2. loud noise

_____

- - - - - - - - - - - - - - - -

_____

3. wet dog

_____

- - - - - - - - - - - - - - - -

_____

4. two girls

_____

- - - - - - - - - - - - - - - -

_____

5. blue water

_____

- - - - - - - - - - - - - - - -

_____

6. funny clown

_____

- - - - - - - - - - - - - - - -

_____

Unit 1
Core Skills Language Arts, Grade 1

Name _____ Date _____

Describing Words About Feelings

Some describing words tell how people **feel**.
Examples: Yesterday Sandi was **sad**.
Now Sandi is **happy**.

**Complete each sentence. Choose a word from the box.
Write it on the line.**

| hungry | sleepy | glad | sick | angry |

1. When Freddy is _____, he takes a nap.

2. When Freddy is _____, he goes to the doctor.

3. When Freddy is _____, he eats.

4. When Freddy sees his friend, he is _____.

5. When Freddy is _____, he is not happy.

Unit 1
Core Skills Language Arts, Grade 1

Name _____   Date _____

Describing Words About Size and Shape

> Some describing words tell about **size** and **shape**.
> *Examples:*   **big** dog
> **square** book

Answer each question. Choose a word in ( ). Write the word on the line.

1. What size is a whale? _____
   (sad, big)

2. What size is an ant? _____
   (small, sleepy)

3. What size is a tree? _____
   (green, tall)

4. What shape is a ball? _____
   (round, blue)

Write a sentence. Use a describing word about size or shape.

5. _____

Describing Words About Color

Some describing words tell about **color**.
Examples: **blue** water
black cat
gray whale

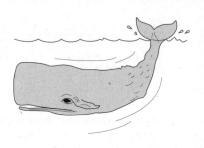

Complete each sentence. Choose a describing word from the box. Write the word on the line.

blue	yellow	pink	white	green	red

1. The grass is _____.

2. The flowers are _____.

3. That bird is bright _____.

4. Watch it fly into the _____ sky.

5. It is flying into a _____ cloud.

6. I am flying a _____ kite.

Describing Words About Numbers

Some describing words tell **how many**.
Examples: **one** nose
              five toes

Complete each sentence. Use a number word from the box.
Use the picture to help you.

one	two	three	four	five
six	seven	eight	nine	ten

1. I have _____ box of milk.

2. I have _____ cookies.

3. I see _____ balloons.

4. The cake has _____ candles.

5. I see _____ pumpkins.

Name _____ Date _____

Describing Words About Taste and Smell

Some describing words tell how things **taste**.

Some describing words tell how things **smell**.
Examples: This is **salty** popcorn.
The flower smells **sweet**.

Circle each describing word. Then, write it on the line.

_____

1. The lemons taste sour. _____

2. The bread smells fresh. _____

3. I like salty peanuts. _____

4. I smell a smoky fire. _____

Write a sentence. Use a describing word about taste or smell.

_____

5. _____

Unit 1
Core Skills Language Arts, Grade 1

Describing Words About Feel and Sound

Some describing words tell how things **feel**.

Some describing words tell how things **sound**.
Examples: Ice cream feels **cold**.
The school bell is **loud**.

Complete each sentence. Choose a word in ( ) that tells about feel or sound. Write the word on the line.

1. The kitten is _____.
(soft, small)

2. I like to read in _____ rooms.
(two, quiet)

3. The sunshine is _____.
(long, hot)

4. I put _____ ice in my drink.
(cold, tall)

5. The ticking clock is _____.
(wet, noisy)

Describing Words About the Weather

Some describing words tell about the **weather**.
Example: We had **stormy** weather **yesterday**.

Look at each picture. Complete each sentence. Choose a weather word from the box. Write it on the line.

rainy	snowy	sunny	windy	cloudy

1. It is a _____ day.

2. It is a _____ day.

3. It is a _____ day.

4. It is a _____ day.

5. It is a _____ day.

Unit 1
Core Skills Language Arts, Grade 1

Using Describing Words

Remember that describing words tell about naming words.

Write a describing word for each naming word.

1.   toad

_____

- - - - - - - - - - - -

_____

4.   whale

_____

- - - - - - - - - - - -

_____

2.   cow

_____

- - - - - - - - - - - -

_____

5.   lion

_____

- - - - - - - - - - - -

_____

3.   chick

_____

- - - - - - - - - - - -

_____

6.   rabbit

_____

- - - - - - - - - - - -

_____

Unit 1
Core Skills Language Arts, Grade 1

Name _____ Date _____

Describing Words That Compare

Some describing words tell how things are different. Add
er to a describing word to tell how two things are different.

Some describing words tell how more than two things are
different. Add est to a describing word to tell how more than
two things are different.

Examples: small, smaller, smallest

The cat is **small**.

The mouse is **smaller** than the cat.

The ant is the **smallest** of all.

**Complete each sentence. Choose the correct comparing
word in ( ). Write the word on the line.**

1. The cat is _____ than the dog.
    (smaller, smallest)

2. The dog is _____ than the cat.
    (bigger, biggest)

3. The elephant is the _____ of all.
    (big, biggest)

4. I am _____ than my brother.
    (tall, taller)

More Describing Words That Compare

Remember that <u>er</u> is used to compare two things and <u>est</u> is used to compare more than two things.

Answer each question. Circle the correct picture.

1. Which goat is <u>bigger</u>?

 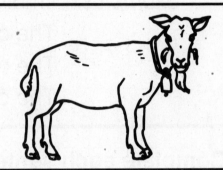

2. Which bridge is <u>longer</u>?

3. Which is the <u>tallest</u> tree of all?

4. Which is the <u>highest</u> building of all?

Unit 1
Core Skills Language Arts, Grade 1

Name _____ Date _____

Using A and An

Use <u>a</u> before words that begin with a consonant sound.

Use <u>an</u> before words that begin with a vowel sound.
The vowels are <u>a</u>, <u>e</u>, <u>i</u>, <u>o</u>, and <u>u</u>.

Examples: **a** car, **a** skate

an ant, **an** egg

Read each word. Write <u>a</u> or <u>an</u> on the line.

1. _____ tent

2. _____ train

3. _____ orange

4. _____ owl

5. _____ book

6. _____ bike

7. _____ apple

8. _____ oak tree

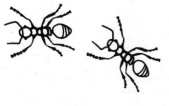   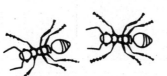 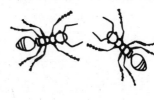

Unit 1
Core Skills Language Arts, Grade 1

Joining Words

Some words join words or ideas.

Use <u>and</u> to join words or ideas that are equal.

Use <u>or</u> to show a choice.

Use <u>but</u> to show differences.

Use <u>because</u> to give a reason.

Examples: Mom baked a pie <u>and</u> a cake.

I can have a slice of pie <u>or</u> cake.

I wanted to have both, <u>but</u> I was too full.

I had cake <u>because</u> it was my birthday.

Complete each sentence. Circle the correct joining word in ( ).

1. I put a coat on (because, or) it was cold outside.

2. We can watch TV (or, but) a movie.

3. Pepe (and, or) Kate are friends.

4. Jill wants some milk, (because, but) the store doesn't have any.

Write words to complete the sentence.

5. I like to eat _____ and

_____ .

Name _____ Date _____

Prepositions

Some words tell where and when.
Examples: The frog is **on** the log.
The frog jumps **toward** me.

Complete each sentence. Use a word from the box.

in	under	toward	on	during

1. The cat is looking _____ the box.

2. The cat sat _____ the chair.

3. The cat is _____ the chair.

4. I hold a balloon _____ the parade.

5. The turtle walks _____ the boy.

Unit 1
Core Skills Language Arts, Grade 1

Unit 2: Sentences
Sentences

A **sentence** is a group of words. It tells a complete idea.

A sentence begins with a capital letter.

Examples: I have two eyes.
Do you have a nose?

Underline the groups of words that are sentences.

1. I see a lion.

see a lion.

2. throws the ball.

Jan throws the ball.

3. I hear a bird.

a bird.

Write the sentences correctly.

4. my cat can jump.

_____

- -

_____

5. the dog barks.

_____

- -

_____

Is It a Sentence?

> Remember that a sentence tells a complete idea.
>
> A sentence begins with a capital letter.

Read each group of words. Write <u>yes</u> if the words are a sentence. Write <u>no</u> if the words are not a sentence.

_____

_____ **1.** Today is my birthday.

_____ **2.** have a party.

_____ **3.** open the presents.

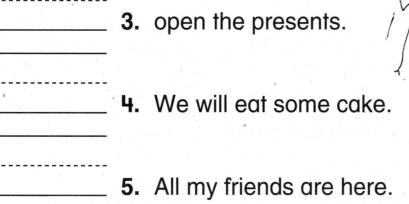

_____ **4.** We will eat some cake.

_____ **5.** All my friends are here.

_____ **6.** play some games.

_____ **7.** making ice cream.

_____ **8.** My birthday party is fun.

Sentence Parts

A sentence has two parts. The **naming part** tells who or what the sentence is about.

The **telling part** tells what someone or something does.

A naming part and a telling part make a complete sentence.

Examples:

Naming Part	Telling Part
Sari	plants some seeds.
The girls	sing a song.

Underline the naming part in each sentence.

1. A frog jumped in the grass.

2. A cat saw the frog.

3. A dog ran after the cat.

Circle the telling part in each sentence.

4. Dogs chew bones.

5. Birds eat worms.

6. Jacy walks to school.

Naming Parts of Sentences

A sentence has a **naming part**. It tells who or what the sentence is about.

Examples: **The friends** play.   **The duck** is brown.

Read each sentence. Then, read the question. Write the answer to the question on the line.

1. Rick went to the zoo.

_____

Who did something? _____

2. His mother went with him.

_____

Who did something? _____

3. The bear ate some food.

_____

What did something? _____

4. The monkey did some tricks.

_____

What did something? _____

5. The tiger slept in its cage.

_____

What did something? _____

Naming Parts of Sentences, part 2

Remember that the naming part tells who or what the sentence is about.

Complete each sentence. Write a naming part. Use the words in the box.

Who	**What**
My sister	The blue kite
Amy	The wind
	The red kite

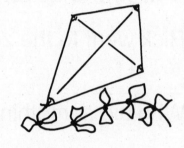

_____

1. _____ flies a blue kite.

2. _____ has a red kite.

3. _____ takes the kites up.

4. _____ is hard to see.

5. _____ is easy to see.

Telling Parts of Sentences

A sentence has a **telling part**. It tells what someone or something does or is.

Examples: Pat **plays in the grass**.
The grass **is green and tall**.

Read each sentence. Then, read the question. Write the answer to the question on the line.

1. Anna found a puppy. What did Anna do?

_____

_____

2. The puppy ate some food. What did the puppy do?

_____

_____

3. The puppy played with Anna. What did the puppy do?

_____

_____

4. Anna named the puppy Skip. What did Anna do?

_____

_____

5. Anna threw the ball. What did Anna do?

_____

_____

Telling Parts of Sentences, part 2

Remember that the telling part tells what someone or something does or is.

Complete each sentence. Write a telling part. Use the words in the box.

Telling Parts
will show you
are fun to grow
gives them light
plant seeds
waters the seeds

1. Flowers _____.

2. I _____.

3. You _____.

4. The rain _____.

5. The sun _____.

Name _____ Date _____

Writing Sentences with Naming Parts

Remember that the naming part tells who or what the sentence is about.

Complete each sentence. Write a naming part.

1. _____ has a bike.

2. _____ is green.

3. _____ is tall.

4. _____ found a pretty rock.

5. _____ reads a book.

6. _____ climbs a tree.

7. _____ barks at a cat.

8. _____ runs to the store.

Unit 2
Core Skills Language Arts, Grade 1

Name _____ Date _____

Writing Sentences with Telling Parts

> Remember that the telling part tells what someone or something does or is.

Complete each sentence. Write a telling part.

1. The man _____ .

2. The cat _____ .

3. The fish _____ .

4. The balloon _____ .

5. My friend _____ .

6. The bird _____ .

7. The boy _____ .

8. The girl _____ .

Simple Sentences

A **simple sentence** has one naming part and one telling part. It tells a complete idea. It starts with a capital letter.

Examples:

Naming Part	**Telling Part**
Meg and Ken	see a zebra.
I	walk to school.
The red car	goes fast.

Answer each question with a complete simple sentence. Be sure your sentence has a naming part and a telling part.

1. What is your name?

_____

- -

_____

2. How old are you?

_____

- -

_____

3. What color do you like best?

_____

- -

_____

4. What food do you like?

_____

- -

_____

Compound Sentences

A **compound sentence** is made of two simple sentences put together. The two parts are joined with a comma **(,)** and a joining word. These are some joining words.

and   but   or   so

Two Simple Sentences	**One Compound Sentence**
I am fast. Joe is faster.	I am fast, <u>but</u> Joe is faster.
Rob rakes the leaves. I put them in bags.	Rob rakes the leaves, <u>and</u> I put them in bags.

Join the sentences. Use a comma (,) and a joining word from the box.

and	but	or	so

1. Meg goes to the park. Al goes to the beach.

_____

_____

2. I like peaches. I don't like plums.

_____

_____

3. It is time for bed. I put on my pajamas.

_____

_____

Word Order in Sentences

Words in a sentence are in order. The words must be in order to make sense.

Example: book a Pablo gets. (makes no sense)

Pablo gets a book. (makes sense)

Write each sentence in correct word order.

1. fast Jim swims

_____

- -

_____.

2. can not swim Jane

_____

- -

_____.

3. Mike art likes

_____

- -

_____.

4. to town Eva walks

_____

- -

_____.

5. Kim bird sees a

_____

- -

_____.

Telling Sentences

A **telling sentence** tells about something or someone. A telling sentence can also give an order. It begins with a capital letter. It ends with a **period (.)**.

Examples: A frog hops away.
We try to get it.
Put your toys away.

Write each telling sentence correctly.

1. i have a pig

_____

- -

_____

2. he and I play

_____

- -

_____

3. get the ball

_____

- -

_____

4. give the ball to me

_____

- -

_____

5. we have fun

_____

- -

_____

Yelling Sentences

A **yelling sentence** shows strong feelings or excitement. It begins with a capital letter. It ends with an exclamation point **(!)**.

Examples: <u>W</u>e are getting a kitten!
<u>L</u>ook at the shooting star!

Write each yelling sentence correctly.

1. we are going to the zoo today

_____

- -

_____

2. look at the giant tiger

_____

- -

_____

3. the lion roared

_____

- -

_____

4. i am so excited

_____

- -

_____

5. i had a great time

_____

- -

_____

Asking Sentences

An **asking sentence** asks about something or someone. It begins with a capital letter. It ends with a **question mark (?)**.

Examples: How old are you?
Do you like pets?

Write each asking sentence correctly.

1. what is your name

_____

- -

_____

2. where do you live

_____

- -

_____

3. when is your birthday

_____

- -

_____

4. do you have a pet

_____

- -

_____

5. who is your best friend

_____

- -

_____

Asking Sentences, part 2

Remember that an asking sentence asks about something or someone. An asking sentence often begins with a question word.

Examples: **What** are you doing?

Where have you been?

Complete each sentence. Write a question word from the box.

Question Words
Who
What
When
Where

_____
----

1. _____ did the circus come to town?
_____
----

2. _____ took you to the circus?
_____
----

3. _____ did you see first?
_____
----

4. _____ are the elephants?
_____
----

5. _____ climbs the rope?

55

Name _____ Date _____

Telling, Asking, or Yelling?

Remember that a telling sentence tells about something or someone. An asking sentence asks about something or someone. A yelling sentence shows strong feelings or excitement.

Examples: I have a new pencil.
When did you get it?
I love that pencil!

Read each sentence. Write tell if it is a telling sentence. Write ask if it is an asking sentence. Write yell it if it is a yelling sentence.

_____

1. I saw a fish.

_____

2. Where did you see it?

_____

3. I saw it in the lake.

_____

4. How big was the fish?

_____

5. The fish was huge!

_____

6. The water is so cold!

Joining Naming Parts

A sentence has a naming part. Sometimes the naming parts of two sentences can be joined. Use the word <u>and</u> to join the parts.

Example: **Turtle** looked. **Fox** looked.
          Turtle <u>and</u> **Fox** looked.

Join the naming parts of the sentences. Use the word <u>and</u>. Write the new sentences.

1. Turtle hid. Fox hid.

_____

- -

_____

2. Jon played ball. Teri played ball.

_____

- -

_____

3. Brett ate lunch. Max ate lunch.

_____

- -

_____

4. Cat played with Duck. Frog played with Duck.

_____

- -

_____

Joining Telling Parts

A sentence has a telling part. Sometimes the telling parts of two sentences can be joined. Use the word <u>and</u> to join the parts.

Example: The birds **fly**. The birds **sing**.
                    The birds **fly and sing**.

Join the telling parts of the sentences. Use the word <u>and</u>. Write the new sentences.

1. Chet reads. Chet writes.

_____

- -

_____

2. The ducks swim. The ducks quack.

_____

- -

_____

3. I found a coin. I found a comb.

_____

- -

_____

4. We will eat some cake. We will eat some ice cream.

_____

- -

_____

- -

_____

Unit 3: Mechanics
Beginning Sentences with a Capital Letter

A sentence always begins with a capital letter.

Examples: The horse ran away.
               A dog ran after the horse.
               I ran after the dog.

Write each sentence correctly. Be sure to begin each sentence with a capital letter.

1. the sun is hot.

_____

- -

_____

2. we found a ring!

_____

- -

_____

3. you can come with us.

_____

- -

_____

4. i will get some water.

_____

- -

_____

The Word I

The word I is always written with a capital letter.

Examples: **I** have a new bike.
Tomorrow **I** will ride to school.
Where can **I** find a flower?

Answer the questions. Write sentences. Begin each sentence with I can.

1. What can you ride?

_____

_ _

_____

2. What can you make?

_____

_ _

_____

3. How can you help at home?

_____

_ _

_____

4. What can you write?

_____

_ _

_____

Writing Names

The names of people and pets always begin with a capital letter. The first letter in each name is a capital letter.

Examples: **C**arla **C**antu   **W**inky
              Yuko **I**to   **S**ilver
              Aunt **A**ngela   **R**in **T**in **T**in
              Uncle **B**art   **F**luffy

Rewrite each name. Begin each name with a capital letter.

1. pat long

_____

2. eva ramos

_____

3. uncle thomas

_____

4. lucky

_____

5. ling chung

_____

6. socks

_____

Writing Names of the Days

The names of the days of the week begin with a capital letter. The first letter in each name is a capital letter.

Examples: **S**unday   **M**onday

Tuesday   **W**ednesday

Thursday   **F**riday

Saturday

August						
Sun	Mon	Tues	Wed	Thur	Fri	Sat
			1	2	3	4
5	6	7	8	9	10	11
12	13	14	15	16	17	18
19	20	21	22	23	24	25
26	27	28	29	30	31	

Read each item. Write the name of a day of the week. Begin each name with a capital letter.

1. Day before Tuesday _____

2. Day after Thursday _____

3. Day before Monday _____

4. Starts with the letter W _____

5. Two days that start with the letter T

_____   _____

Name _____ Date _____

Writing Names of the Months

The names of the months of the year begin with a capital letter. The first letter in each name is a capital letter.

Examples: **J**une   **A**ugust   **N**ovember

Read the name of the month. Then, rewrite the name. Begin the name with a capital letter.

1. january

2. february

3. march

4. may

5. july

6. august

7. september

8. october

9. november

10. december

Writing Names of Holidays

The names of holidays begin with a capital letter. The first letter in each important part of the name is a capital letter.

Examples: **N**ew **Y**ear's **D**ay
Fourth of **J**uly
Earth **D**ay

Read each sentence. Write the name of each holiday correctly. Begin each important part of the name with a capital letter.

1. I get cards on valentine's day.

_____

- -

_____

2. Let's plant a tree on arbor day.

_____

- -

_____

3. Dad likes independence day.

_____

- -

_____

4. Did you go away on thanksgiving day?

_____

- -

_____

Name _____ Date _____

Writing Names of Special Places

The names of special places begin with a capital letter. Some special places are streets, cities, and states. The first letter in each part of the name is a capital letter.

Examples: **F**irst **S**treet **N**ew **Y**ork **C**ity **F**lorida

Read each sentence. Underline the names of streets, cities, or states. Then, rewrite each sentence correctly. Use capital letters where they are needed.

1. Billy lives on jane street.

_____

- -

_____

2. My uncle lives on river road.

_____

- -

_____

3. I live on lake drive.

_____

- -

_____

4. Diane lives in boston.

_____

- -

_____

Writing Titles of Books

Begin the first word, last word, and all important words in a book title with a capital letter. Underline the title of a book.

Examples: <u>T</u>he <u>S</u>ilver <u>P</u>ony
<u>P</u>eas at <u>S</u>upper
<u>B</u>illy and <u>B</u>laze

Rewrite each title correctly. Use capital letters where they are needed. Underline each title that you write.

1. red flags

_____

- -

_____

2. the black horse

_____

- -

_____

3. dad and me

_____

- -

_____

4. flowers for mom

_____

- -

_____

Period

Use a **period (.)** at the end of a telling sentence.

Examples: I can swing.

The slide is tall.

Write each sentence correctly.

1. The bears play a game

_____

2. They throw a ball

_____

3. A bear came home

_____

4. Frog came to visit

_____

Question Mark and Exclamation Point

Use a **question mark (?)** at the end of asking sentences.
Example: Will it rain today**?**

Use an **exclamation point (!)** at the end of yelling sentences.
Example: The sky is very dark**!**

Write each asking or yelling sentence correctly.

1. Why is the sky blue

---

2. How do flowers grow

---

3. I see a rocket in the sky

---

4. Look at the colorful bird

---

5. When will the sun shine

Comma

> Use a **comma (,)** between the day and the year in a date.
>
> *Examples:*   July 4, 1776   November 18, 2009

JUNE
1

Read each sentence. Circle the date. Then, write the date correctly. Remember to use a capital letter to begin the name of the month.

1. I got a letter on may 23 2012.

_____

- -

_____

2. Jan had a party on january 1 2014.

_____

- -

_____

3. Kim was born on june 30 2008.

_____

- -

_____

4. Leo got a new puppy on october 31 2013.

_____

- -

_____

Complete the sentence with today's date.

_____

- -

5. Today is _____.

More Commas

> Use a **comma (,)** between three or more words in a list.
> Use <u>and</u> before the last word in the list.
>
> *Examples:*   We have apples, peaches, and pears.
>   I like red, green, yellow, and blue.
>   Mom, Dad, and Ken are in the kitchen.

Read each sentence. Add commas between the words in the lists. Write the sentence correctly.

1. I can run jump and skip.

----

2. The zoo has lions bears zebras and monkeys.

----

3. Cars trucks and buses drive on the road.

----

4. Ana Emma and Maria play the game.

----

5. Frank packed pants shirts and socks.

Name _____   Date _____

Spelling

These rules can help you spell many words correctly. Use the letter i before e, except after c.

Examples: friend   piece   field

If a word ends in a consonant plus y, change the y to i before adding ed or es.

Examples: baby → babies   city → cities

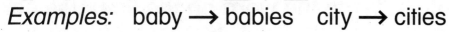
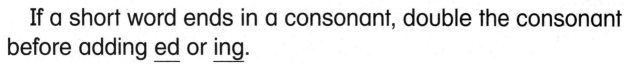

If a short word ends in a consonant, double the consonant before adding ed or ing.

Examples: hop → hopped   sit → sitting

Complete each sentence. Choose the word that is spelled correctly. Write it on the line.

_____

1. Tara is my _____.
(friend, freind)

_____

2. We are _____ to the park.
(skiping, skipping)

_____

3. Now we pass a soccer _____.
(feild, field)

_____

4. Tara _____ to the swings.
(hurrys, hurries)

Spelling, part 2

Many words that end with a long vowel sound and a consonant are spelled with an e at the end. The letter e is silent.

Examples: hope   make   bite   time

Look at each picture. Write the word on the line. Use correct spelling.

1.

_____

- - - - - - - - - - - - - - - -

_____

4.

_____

- - - - - - - - - - - - - - - -

_____

2.

_____

- - - - - - - - - - - - - - - -

_____

5.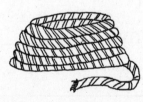

_____

- - - - - - - - - - - - - - - -

_____

3.

_____

- - - - - - - - - - - - - - - -

_____

6.

_____

- - - - - - - - - - - - - - - -

_____

Unit 3
Core Skills Language Arts, Grade 1

Unit 4: Vocabulary and Usage
Rhyming Words

Words that end with the same sounds are **rhyming words**. Here are some rhyming words.

Examples: car—star boat—goat top—drop

Read each sentence. Look at the word in dark print. Choose the word in ( ) that ends with the same sound. Write the rhyming word on the line.

1. It is lots of **fun**

   _____

   to play in the _____.
   (sand, sun)

2. I can run and **hide**

   _____

   and go down the _____.
   (slide, sled)

3. Our new gray **cat**

   _____

   lay on a soft _____.
   (mat, mop)

4. The little black **bug**

   _____

   went under the _____.
   (rag, rug)

Words That Mean the Same

Some words mean almost the same thing.
Examples: small—little   hop—jump

Read each sentence. Look at the word in dark print. Choose a word from the box that means almost the same thing. Write the word on the line.

catch	road	big	home

_____

----

1. The man left his **house**. _____

_____

----

2. He walked down the **street**. _____

_____

----

3. The dog could not **get** him. _____

_____

----

4. The dog was **large**. _____

Name _____ Date _____

Words That Mean the Same, part 2

Remember that some words mean almost the same thing.

Example: look—watch

Read each pair of sentences. Look at the word in dark print in the first sentence. Circle a word in the second sentence that means almost the same thing. Write both words on the line.

1. I hear a **sound**. The noise is my puppy.

_____

_____

2. I **begin** to call his name. My puppy starts to bark.

_____

_____

3. I **look** under my bed. I see him there.

_____

_____

4. He is **glad** to see me. I am happy, too.

_____

_____

5. My puppy is **little**. He is a small dog.

_____

_____

Unit 4
Core Skills Language Arts, Grade 1

Words That Mean the Opposite

Some words have opposite meanings.
Example: happy—sad

Read each sentence. Look at the word in dark print.
Circle the word in ( ) that means the opposite.

1. Pete went **up** the stairs. (down, out)

2. He sat on his **soft** bed. (new, hard)

3. Soon it was **dark** outside. (light, cold)

4. He turned **on** the lamp. (red, off)

5. Pete looked **out** the window. (in, off)

6. He **closed** his eyes. (rubbed, opened)

7. Soon Pete was **asleep**. (hungry, awake)

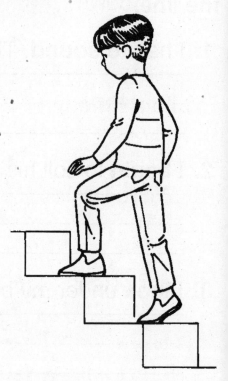

Words That Mean the Opposite, part 2

Remember that some words have opposite meanings.
Examples: up—down   hot—cold

Read each sentence. Look at the word in dark print. Choose a word from the box that means the opposite. Write the word on the line.

| down | in | big | new | soft | off |

_____
- -

1. I am **little**, and my sister is _____.

_____
- -

2. When I go **out**, she comes _____.

_____
- -

3. Her bike is **old**, but mine is _____.

_____
- -

4. First I get **on** my bike, then I get _____.

_____
- -

5. I go **up** the steps and _____ the slide.

6. The apple is **hard**, and the cookie is

_____
- -

_____.

Unit 4
Core Skills Language Arts, Grade 1

Words That Sound Alike

Some words sound alike, but they have different meanings.

Examples: hear—here   there—their

Read each pair of sentences. Circle the words in each pair that sound alike.

1. I know what Jane said.
She told her dog "no."

2. I yelled "hi" to Bill.
He waved to me from a high window.

3. I had eight bugs.
My frog ate seven of them.

4. Mom bakes cookies with flour.
She draws a flower with pink icing.

5. I love to go to the sea.
I like to see the boats.

6. My mother went to a sale.
She got a sail for my boat.

7. I read a story yesterday.
It was about a red dog.

8. I cannot hear you.
Come over here.

78

Words That Sound Alike, part 2

Some words sound alike, but they have different meanings. <u>To</u> and <u>two</u> sound alike, but they mean different things.

Examples: I went **to** my aunt's house.
   She gave me **two** gifts.

Complete each sentence. Circle the correct word in ( ).

1. I took a ball (to, two) Ben.

2. Now he has (to, two) balls.

3. Ben went (to, two) the game.

4. He ate (to, two) hot dogs.

5. He wants (to, two) play ball.

6. I have (to, two) hands.

7. I used them (to, two) clap.

8. My house has (to, two) doors.

Choosing the Right Meaning

Some words are spelled alike, but they have different meanings.

Examples:

roll—kind of bread   I had a **roll** for lunch.

roll—turn over and over   I like to **roll** down the hill.

Read each sentence. Look at the word in dark print. Then, draw a line to the correct picture meaning.

1. Tony hit the ball with a **bat**.

2. The **bat** flies in the dark.   **a.**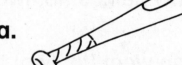

3. Juan plays ball with a heavy **bat**.

4. How does a **bat** see at night?   **b.**

5. The **duck** made a loud quack.

6. We had to **duck** under the fence.   **a.**

7. We were asked to **duck** so they could see.   **b.**

8. The **duck** swam in the water.

Choosing the Right Word

Some words mean almost the same. Choose words that best fit the meaning.

Examples: The toad <u>hops</u> over the twig.
I <u>jump</u> over the stick.
The deer <u>leaps</u> over the log.

Read the sentences. Circle the word in ( ) that best matches the meaning.

1. You hear a strange sound.
You (stare, peek) into the closet.

2. Ted was angry.
He (stomped, walked) down the stairs.

3. Tina saw the tallest building in the world.
The building was (big, gigantic).

4. Karen wants to win the race.
She (runs, jogs) to the finish line.

5. Alan scored the winning goal.
He is (glad, thrilled).

Prefixes

A **prefix** is a word part at the beginning of a word. A prefix changes the meaning of the word.

The prefix <u>re</u> means "again."

The prefix <u>un</u> means "not."

Examples: I am <u>happy</u>. Greg is <u>unhappy</u>.

Raj <u>plays</u> the song. Then Raj <u>replays</u> the song.

Look at the word in dark print. Circle the meaning of the word.

1. The rules are **unfair**.
(not fair, to be fair again)

2. Mom will **rewash** my jeans.
(wash again, not wash)

3. I **relock** the door.
(not lock, lock again)

4. The words are **unclear**.
(clear again, not clear)

5. I will **rewrite** my story.
(not write, write again)

Unit 4
Core Skills Language Arts, Grade 1

Name _____ Date _____

Suffixes

A **suffix** is a word part at the end of a word. A suffix changes the meaning of the word.

The suffix <u>less</u> means "without."

The suffix <u>ful</u> means "full of."

Examples: Patty is <u>thankful</u> for the help she gets.
                  The dog has a loud bark, but it is <u>harmless</u>.

Look at the word in dark print. Circle the meaning of the word.

1. Please be **careful** with the glass vase.
   (full of care, without care)

2. Zack can see the moon and stars in
   the **cloudless** sky.
   (full of clouds, without clouds)

3. We are **hopeful** that our team will win.
   (full of hope, without hope)

4. Our cat is **fearless** when she jumps.
   (without fear, full of fear)

5. Kim is a **cheerful** girl.
   (full of cheer, without cheer)

Unit 4
Core Skills Language Arts, Grade 1

Root Words

A **root word** is the main part of a word. Sometimes letters are added to the beginning or end of a root word.

Examples: Ray <u>look</u>ed under his bed.
Now he <u>look</u>s in the closet.
Ray is <u>look</u>ing for his hat.

Look at the word in dark print. Find the root word. Write the root word on the line.

1. Manny **talked** to his teacher.
_____

_____

2. Emily **brings** her backpack.
_____

_____

3. Sharon is **running** on the track.
_____

_____

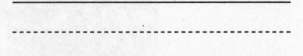

4. Omar **gives** the toy to his brother.
_____

_____

5. Dad **passed** the salt to Mom.
_____

_____

Context Clues

Context clues help you find the meaning
of an unknown word. Use the other words in
a sentence to guess the meaning.

Example: The <u>infant</u> sleeps in a crib and cries a lot.

↑   ↑
clue   clue

The context clues help you guess that an
<u>infant</u> is a <u>baby</u>.

**Look at the word in dark print. Look for context clues in the
sentence. Circle the meaning of the word.**

1. For dinner, we ate a **feast** of turkey, salad, stuffing, and pie.
   (big meal, large table)

2. The **enormous** wave was thirty feet tall
   when it crashed over the ship.
   (wet, huge)

3. The snake **slithered** across the ground.
   (crawled, flew)

4. Pablo **penned** a letter to Grandma and mailed it.
   (watched, wrote)

5. A big **downpour** flooded the streets and made big puddles
   in our yard.
   (heavy rainfall, large fire)

Words That Show Order

Some words tell about **order**. Some order words are <u>first</u>, <u>next</u>, <u>then</u>, and <u>last</u>.

Example:

| first | next | then | last |

Complete the story. Use the words <u>First</u>, <u>Next</u>, <u>Then</u>, and <u>Last</u>.

Jack the Panda had a loose tooth.

_____

_____ he wiggled his tooth.

_____ it fell out.

_____ he put his tooth under his pillow.

_____ he found a toy under his pillow.

Compound Words

A **compound word** is made of two words. The two words are put together to make a new word.

Examples:

song + bird = songbird

bed + room = bedroom

every + thing = everything

Complete each sentence. Use a compound word from the box.

| sandbox | treehouse | backyard | birdhouse |

1. There are two trees in my _____.

2. My dad built a _____ in one tree.

3. There is a _____ in the other tree.

4. I like to play in my _____.

Unit 5: Writing
Writing Sentences

A sentence tells a complete idea. A sentence begins with a capital letter. It has a naming part and a telling part.

Naming Part	Telling Part
The children	rode a bus to school.

Look at the sentence parts in the box. Draw a line from a naming part to a telling part. Then, write the sentence on the line. Be sure to put a period at the end of the sentence.

Naming Part	Telling Part
1. The birds	digs
2. That frog	swims
3. The fish	hops
4. My dog	fly

1. _____

2. _____

3. _____

4. _____

Writing Sentences with Naming Words

A sentence is a group of words. It tells a complete idea. A sentence begins with a capital letter.

A naming word tells about a person, place, or thing.

Example: The black **dog** barks.

Complete each sentence. Choose a naming word from the box. Write it on the line.

| flowers | garden | rain | seeds | store | sun |

1. Jo went to the _____.

2. She got some little brown _____.

3. Jo will plant the seeds in the _____.

4. The _____ will fall on the garden.

5. The _____ will warm the garden.

6. Pretty _____ will grow in the garden.

Writing Sentences with Action Words

A sentence tells a complete idea. A sentence begins with a capital letter.

An action word tells what something or someone does.
Example: Barry **drinks** some juice.

Complete each sentence. Choose an action word from the box. Write it on the line.

bark	climbs	chase	eat	jump	run

_____

\-

1. The two dogs _____ fast.

_____

\-

2. The dogs _____ up.

_____

\-

3. They _____ their food.

_____

\-

4. The dogs _____ the cat.

_____

\-

5. The dogs _____ loudly.

_____

\-

6. The cat _____ a tree.

Name _____ Date _____

Writing Sentences with Describing Words

Describing words make sentences more interesting.

Example: I saw a flower.

I saw a **pink** flower.

Complete each sentence. Add describing words.

_____

- -

1. Ice cream is _____ .

_____

- -

2. I ate a _____ apple.

_____

- -

3. I have _____ pencils.

_____

- -

4. The dog is _____ .

_____

- -

5. The cat is _____ .

_____

- -

6. The rabbit is _____ and

_____

- -

_____ .

Unit 5
Core Skills Language Arts, Grade 1

Writing More Sentences

A sentence tells a complete idea. It begins with a capital letter. A telling sentence ends with a period.

Example: I am resting.

Write a telling sentence to answer each question.

1. Are you a girl or a boy?

_____

- -

_____

2. Are you sitting or standing?

_____

- -

_____

3. Do you use a pen or a pencil?

_____

- -

_____

4. Do you walk or ride to school?

_____

- -

_____

5. Is it day or night now?

_____

- -

_____

Writing Sentences About a Picture

A sentence tells a complete idea. It begins with a capital letter. It has a naming part and a telling part.

Look at the picture carefully. Then, write at least three sentences that tell about the picture.

_____

_____

_____

_____

_____

_____

Paragraphs

A **paragraph** is a group of sentences. The sentences tell about one main idea. The first line of a paragraph is indented. This means the first word is moved in a little from the left edge.

The first sentence in a paragraph tells the main idea. The other sentences tell about the main idea.

Example:

Red Creek School is finished. The inside is nice and bright. The playground is very big. The school will open very soon. You will like the new school.

How to Write a Paragraph

1. Write a sentence that tells the main idea.

2. Indent the first line.

3. Write sentences that tell more about the main idea.

Write sentences that tell about this main idea.

I like school.

_____

- -

_____

- -

_____

- -

_____

Unit 5
Core Skills Language Arts, Grade 1

Writing a Story About You

A **story about you** is one kind of story you can write. In a story about you, you tell about something you did.

Example:

I like to dive. I practice every day. At the pool I climb the ladder. Then, I walk to the end of the diving board. I put my arms up, and I dive. Splash! Into the water I go.

How to Write a Story About You

1. Think about things you have done.

2. Choose one thing to write about.

3. Begin your story.

4. Tell in order what you did.

5. Use words like I and me.

Answer the question.

What is the main idea of the example story? (Remember, the main idea is the first sentence of the paragraph.)

_____

- -

_____

Writing a Story About You, part 2

Think about something you have done. Write a story about you. Write your main idea in the first sentence. Indent the first sentence. Give your story a title. Draw a picture to go with your story.

_____

- -

_____

- -

_____

- -

_____

- -

_____

- -

_____

Unit 5
Core Skills Language Arts, Grade 1

Writing an Opinion

An **opinion paragraph** tells how you feel about something. It gives reasons why you feel that way.

Example:

Harris Park is a great place to visit. I really like Harris Park. You can do a lot of things there. The park has a nice playground. The playground has swings and slides. The park has a pretty pond with ducks. If you visit Harris Park, you will have a good time.

How to Write an Opinion Paragraph

1. Think about things you like or don't like.

2. Choose one thing to write about.

3. Write a sentence telling what your paragraph is about.

4. Write a sentence that tells how you feel.

5. Write sentences that give reasons why you feel that way.

6. Write an ending sentence.

Answer the question.

What does the example paragraph give an opinion about?

_____

- -

_____

Writing an Opinion, part 2

Think about something you like. Write an opinion paragraph about it. Tell about the thing you like. Give reasons why you like it. Write an ending sentence. Draw a picture to go with your opinion paragraph.

_____

- -

_____

- -

_____

- -

_____

- -

_____

- -

Unit 5
Core Skills Language Arts, Grade 1

Name _____ Date _____

Writing a Description

In a **description**, you tell about something. You use words that tell how the thing looks, sounds, tastes, smells, or feels.

Example:

The Fish Store

Our class went to a fish store. It was small and dark inside. There were many pretty fish. We watched a girl feed the fish. Then they swam fast!

How to Write a Description

1. Think about things you have seen.

2. Choose one to write about.

3. Write a sentence that tells what you are describing.

4. Write sentences that tell what the thing was like.

5. Use describing words. Give details about how the thing looks, sounds, tastes, smells, or feels.

6. Give your description a title.

Complete the sentence.

One describing word in the example story is

_____

_____.

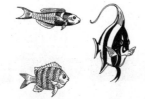 

Writing a Description, part 2

Think about something you have seen. Write a description of it. Use describing words. Write your main idea in the first sentence. Indent the first sentence. Give your description a title. Draw a picture to go with your description.

_____

- -

_____

- -

_____

_____

- -

_____

- -

_____

_____

- -

Writing a Friendly Letter

You can write a **friendly letter** to someone you know. In it, you tell about yourself. A friendly letter has five parts. They are the date, greeting, body, closing, and signature.

Example:

date → July 27, 2003

greeting → Dear Sam,

body → I like my new house. At first I was lonely. Then I met Jake. We played ball. Now he is my friend. And so are you!

closing → Your friend,

signature → Danny

How to Write a Friendly Letter

1. Choose a friend to write to.

2. Write about things you have done.

3. Use capital letters and commas correctly.

4. Use the five parts that are shown by the arrows.

Answer the question.

_____

- -

Who wrote the example letter? _____

Writing a Friendly Letter, part 2

Think about something you have done. Think of a friend to write to in a letter. Write a letter to your friend. Use capital letters and commas correctly. Be sure to use the five parts of a friendly letter.

Writing a How-to Paragraph

A **how-to paragraph** tells how to do or make something. The steps are told in order.

Example:

I can play hide-and-seek. You can play it, too. You will need places to hide. You also need some friends to play with. First, close your eyes. Then, count to ten while your friends hide. Last, go and find your friends.

How to Write a How-To Paragraph

1. Think about things you know how to do.

2. Choose one to write about.

3. Write how to do that thing.

4. Tell the things you will need to do it.

5. Tell the steps in the right order.

6. Use words like <u>first</u> and <u>last</u>.

Answer the question.

What does the example paragraph tell how to do?

_____

- -

_____

Writing a How-to Paragraph, part 2

Think about something you know how to do. Write a paragraph telling how to do it. Write what you will tell about in the first sentence. Indent the first sentence. Tell what is needed to do the thing. Use order words. Draw a picture to go with your how-to paragraph.

_____

_____

_____

_____

_____

Name _____ Date _____

Writing a Book Report

A **book report** tells about a book you have read.
Example:

Birthday Cookies
by Ann Wilson

Birthday Cookies is about Tom. He and his mother bake lots of cookies. Tom takes them to school for his birthday. My favorite part is when the other children eat all the cookies. I really liked this book.

How to Write a Book Report

1. Write the title of the book. Underline it.
2. Write the author's name.
3. Tell who or what the book is about.
4. Tell what happens.
5. Tell your favorite part.
6. Tell what you think about the book.

Answer the question.

What is the title of the book in the book report?

_____

- -

_____

Writing a Book Report, part 2

Think about a book you have read. Write a paragraph telling about the book. Tell the name of the book and who wrote it. Tell what happens in the book. Tell your favorite part. Tell if you liked the book. Indent the first sentence. Draw a picture to go with your book report.

106

Unit 6: Research Skills
ABC Order

The order of letters from A to Z is called **ABC order**.

**a b c d e f g h i j k l m n
o p q r s t u v w x y z**

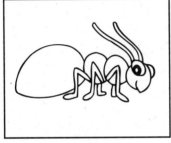

ant

bear

cat

Write the letters in ABC order.

1. a b c
_____ _____ _____

- - - - - - -   - - - - - - -   - - - - - - -

_____ _____ _____

4. p n o
_____ _____ _____

- - - - - - -   - - - - - - -   - - - - - - -

_____ _____ _____

2. f h g
_____ _____ _____

- - - - - - -   - - - - - - -   - - - - - - -

_____ _____ _____

5. i h j
_____ _____ _____

- - - - - - -   - - - - - - -   - - - - - - -

_____ _____ _____

3. c e d
_____ _____ _____

- - - - - - -   - - - - - - -   - - - - - - -

_____ _____ _____

6. z x y
_____ _____ _____

- - - - - - -   - - - - - - -   - - - - - - -

_____ _____ _____

ABC Order, part 2

Use the first letter of a word to put it in ABC order.

Examples: **b**ig   **c**at   **d**og

fish   **m**an   **s**un

Look at each group of words. Look at the letters in dark print. Write the words in ABC order on the lines.

1. a b c d e f

can   **b**ird   **d**ig

_____

_____

_____

_____

3. m n o p q r

red   **o**ne   **n**ame

_____

_____

_____

_____

2. e f g h i j

give   **h**elp   **f**ind

_____

_____

_____

_____

4. s t u v w x

we   **s**he   **t**hey

_____

_____

_____

_____

ABC Order, part 3

Remember that the order of letters from <u>A</u> to <u>Z</u> is called ABC order. Words can be in ABC order, too. Use the first letter of a word to put it in ABC order.

First, number the words in ABC order. Then, write the words in order to make sentences. Be sure to put a period at the end of each sentence.

1. _____ likes   _____ me   _____ He

_____

_____

2. _____ Dave   _____ playing   _____ is

_____

_____

3. _____ outside   _____ Anna   _____ goes

_____

_____

4. _____ Mouse   _____ Cat   _____ finds

_____

_____

Parts of a Book

The **title page** is in the front of a book. It tells the title of the book. It tells who wrote the book. And it tells what company published the book.

Look at this title page from a book about dogs. Then, answer the questions.

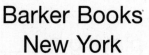

ALL ABOUT DOGS
by
Minnie Fleas

Barker Books
New York

1. What is the title of the book?

_____

_____

2. Who wrote the book?

_____

_____

3. What company published the book?

_____

_____

Parts of a Book, part 2

Some books have many stories or chapters. The **table of contents** of a book tells where each story or chapter begins.

Look at the picture of the book. Write the page number where each chapter begins.

Table of Contents

What Bears Look Like .. 4

Food for Bears 8

Where Bears Live 12

Kinds of Bears 14

1. Food for Bears _____

2. Where Bears Live _____

3. What Bears Look Like _____

4. Kinds of Bears _____

Order of Events

> The sentences in a story tell things in the order they happen.
>
> Words such as <u>first</u>, <u>next</u>, <u>then</u>, and <u>last</u> help tell when things happen.
> *Example:*
>> Brett got ready for bed. **First**, she took a bath. **Next**, she brushed her teeth. **Then**, she put on her pajamas. **Last**, she read a story and got into bed.

Read the story. Then, number the sentences. Write <u>1</u>, <u>2</u>, <u>3</u>, or <u>4</u> to show what happened first, second, third, and last.

Carla planted flowers. First, she got a shovel. Next, she dug some holes in the garden. Then, she put the flowers into the holes. Last, she put the shovel back in its place.

_____

_____ First, she got a shovel.

_____

_____ Then, she put the flowers into the holes.

_____

_____ Last, she put the shovel back in its place.

_____

_____ Next, she dug some holes in the garden.

Conclusions

A **conclusion** is a decision you make. You look at the facts. You think carefully. Then, you decide. You make a conclusion.

Example:

It has many teeth. But it cannot bite. What is it?

Answer: a comb.

Read each animal riddle. Write the name of the animal.

| bird | rabbit | monkey | whale |

1. This animal is very big.
   It lives in the water.
   But it is not a fish.
   What is it?

   _____
   _____

2. This animal can hop fast.
   It has a small, fluffy tail.
   It eats in my garden!
   What is it?

   _____
   _____

3. This animal can climb.
   It has a long tail.
   It lives in the tops of trees.
   What is it?

   _____
   _____

4. This animal can fly.
   It sits on a branch.
   It makes a nest.
   What is it?

   _____
   _____

Classifying

> **Classify** means to put things in groups. Think about how things are alike. Then, you can put them in groups together.

Look at the drawings. Think. How are the animals in each group alike? Write the word.

Animals that _____

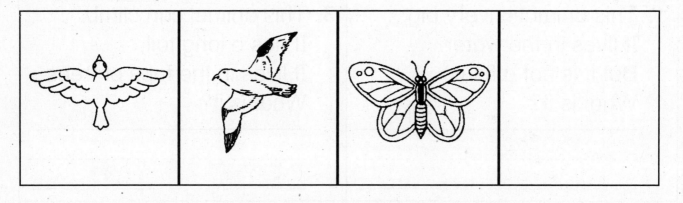

Animals that _____

Draw a picture of another animal for each group.

Categories

A **category** is a kind of group. Things in a category are alike in some way.

Read the words in the box. Write the words in the correct category.

apple	jacket	socks	carrot
shirt	pizza	pants	cupcake

Clothing   **Food**

_____   _____

-                -

_____   _____

-                -

_____   _____

-                -

_____   _____

-                -

Connections

A category is a kind of group. You can make connections between things in a category.

Read each description. Circle the correct word.

1. shoes that you wear in the winter	boots	sandals
2. fruit with a thick peel	banana	apple
3. large cat with striped fur	lion	tiger
4. a large area of water	puddle	lake
5. game that you play with a bat and a ball	baseball	soccer
6. food that is very cold	bread	ice cream

Comparing and Contrasting

Compare means to tell how things are alike. **Contrast** means to tell how things are different.

Look at the two pictures. Think. How are they different? How are they alike? Write one sentence telling how they are alike. Write one sentence telling how they are different.

 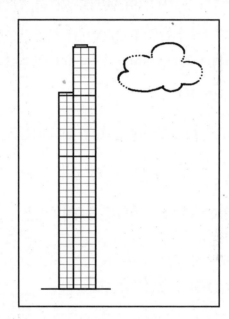

_____

- -

_____

_____

- -

_____

_____

- -

_____

_____

- -

_____

Unit 6
Core Skills Language Arts, Grade 1

Summarizing

> **Summarize** means to tell what happens in a story in your own words.

Read the story. Then, complete the story map.

Matt's Birthday

Matt the Mouse was sad. Today was his birthday. He could not find any of his friends. He went for a walk in the garden. He looked at the plants. They were moving!

"Who is back there?" called Matt.

"Surprise!" shouted all his friends. "Happy birthday, Matt!"

"Thank you!" Matt smiled.

What happened first? _____

_____

What happened next? _____

_____

What happened at the end? _____

_____

Answer Key

page 1
1. boy, 2. girl, 3. dog, 4. cat

page 2
1. doctor, 2. farmer, 3. worker, 4. cook

page 3
Answers may vary. 1. fish, 2. frog, 3. fox, 4. bird, 5. dog, 6. cat

page 4
1. lake, 2. house, 3. park, 4. farm

page 5
1. cup, 2. crayons, 3. apple, 4. bed, 5. hat, 6. box

page 6
1. Chris, 2. Lina, 3. Lee Chin, 4. Main Street, 5. "All About Worms"

page 7
1. dog's, 2. teacher's, 3. Dad's, 4. doll's

page 8
1. birds, 2. bug, 3. girls, 4. dog, 5. frogs

page 9
1. I, 2. me, 3. I, 4. I, 5. me

page 10
1. We are here., 2. They are not here., 3. We will play ball., 4. They found a kitten.

page 11
1. She likes to write., 2. He likes to read., 3. It is on the table., 4. She saw the bird.

page 12
1. Mom and Dad wash their car., 2. The boy plays with his car., 3. I play with her puppy.

page 13
Answers may vary. 1. Nobody, 2. Everybody, 3. Nothing, 4. Everything

page 14
1. eats, 2. waves, 3. talks, 4. sing, 5. ride

page 15
1. swims, 2. hops, 3. crawls, 4. fly

page 16
Answers may vary. Possible responses are given. 1. jump, jumps, 2. roll, rolls, 3. bark, barks

page 17
1. shines, 2. grow, 3. hops, 4. need, 5. gets

page 18
1. played, 2. looked, 3. jumped, 4. walked

page 19
1. will have, 2. will come, 3. will eat, 4. will play

page 20
1. is, 2. is, 3. are, 4. are, 5. are, 6. is

page 21
1. was, 2. were, 3. were, 4. was, 5. was, 6. was

page 22
1. ran, 2. run, 3. saw, 4. came, 5. come, 6–7. Sentences will vary.

page 23
1. went, 2. went, 3. go, 4. went, 5. go, 6. go

page 24
1. don't, 2. won't, 3. can't, 4. isn't, 5. haven't

page 25
Answers may vary. 1. today, 2. outside, 3. always, 4. Soon, 5. inside

page 26
1. green, 2. loud, 3. wet, 4. two, 5. blue, 6. funny

page 27
1. sleepy, 2. sick, 3. hungry, 4. glad, 5. angry

page 28
1. big, 2. small, 3. tall, 4. round, 5. Sentences will vary.

page 29
Answers may vary. 1. green, 2. pink, 3. yellow, 4. blue, 5. white, 6. red

page 30
1. one, 2. four, 3. two, 4. five, 5. seven

page 31
1. sour, 2. fresh, 3. salty, 4. smoky, 5. Sentences will vary.

page 32
1. soft, 2. quiet, 3. hot, 4. cold, 5. noisy

page 33
1. cloudy, 2. snowy, 3. sunny, 4. rainy, 5. windy

page 34
Describing words will vary.

page 35
1. smaller, 2. bigger, 3. biggest, 4. taller

page 36
Check to see that the correct picture is circled.

page 37
1. a, 2. a, 3. an, 4. an, 5. a, 6. a, 7. an, 8. an

page 38
1. because, 2. or, 3. and, 4. but, 5. Answers will vary.

page 39
1. in, 2. on, 3. under, 4. during, 5. toward

page 40
1. I see a lion., 2. Jan throws the ball., 3. I hear a bird.,
4. My cat can jump., 5. The dog barks.

page 41
1. yes, 2. no, 3. no, 4. yes, 5. yes, 6. no, 7. no, 8. yes

page 42
1. A frog, 2. A cat, 3. A dog, 4. chew bones, 5. eat worms,
6. walks to school

page 43
1. Rick, 2. His mother, 3. The bear, 4. The monkey,
5. The tiger

page 44
Answers may vary. 1. My sister, 2. Amy, 3. The wind, 4. The
blue kite, 5. The red kite

page 45
1. found a puppy, 2. ate some food, 3. played with Anna,
4. named the puppy Skip, 5. threw the ball

page 46
Answers may vary. 1. are fun to grow, 2. will show you,
3. plant seeds, 4. waters the seeds, 5. gives them light

page 47
Answers will vary. Be sure that a naming part is given.

page 48
Answers will vary. Be sure that a telling part is given.

page 49
Answers will vary.

page 50
Answers may vary. 1. Meg goes to the park, and Al goes to
the beach., 2. I like peaches, but I don't like plums., 3. It is
time for bed, so I put on my pajamas.

page 51
1. Jim swims fast., 2. Jane can not swim., 3. Mike likes art.,
4. Eva walks to town., 5. Kim sees a bird.

page 52
1. I have a pig., 2. He and I play., 3. Get the ball.,
4. Give the ball to me., 5. We have fun.

page 53
1. We are going to the zoo today!, 2. Look at the giant
tiger!, 3. The lion roared!, 4. I am so excited!, 5. I had a
great time!

page 54
1. What is your name?, 2. Where do you live?, 3. When is
your birthday?, 4. Do you have a pet?, 5. Who is your best
friend?

page 55
Answers may vary. 1. When, 2. Who, 3. What, 4. Where,
5. Who

page 56
1. tell, 2. ask, 3. tell, 4. ask, 5. yell, 6. yell

page 57
1. Turtle and Fox hid., 2. Jon and Teri played ball., 3. Brett
and Max ate lunch., 4. Cat and Frog played with Duck.

page 58
Answers may vary slightly. 1. Chet reads and writes.,
2. The ducks swim and quack., 3. I found a coin and a
comb., 4. We will eat some cake and some ice cream.

page 59
1. The sun is hot., 2. We found a ring!, 3. You can come
with us., 4. I will get some water.

page 60
Answers will vary. Be sure each sentence begins with "I
can."

page 61
1. Pat Long, 2. Eva Ramos, 3. Uncle Thomas, 4. Lucky,
5. Ling Chung, 6. Socks

page 62
1. Monday, 2. Friday, 3. Sunday, 4. Wednesday,
5. Tuesday, Thursday

page 63
1. January, 2. February, 3. March, 4. May, 5. July,
6. August, 7. September, 8. October, 9. November,
10. December

page 64
1. Valentine's Day, 2. Arbor Day, 3. Independence Day,
4. Thanksgiving Day

page 65
1. jane street; Billy lives on Jane Street., 2. river road; My
uncle lives on River Road., 3. lake drive; I live on Lake
Drive., 4. boston; Diane lives in Boston.

page 66
1. Red Flags, 2. The Black Horse, 3. Dad and Me,
4. Flowers for Mom

page 67
1. The bears play a game., 2. They throw a ball., 3. A bear
came home., 4. Frog came to visit.

page 68
1. Why is the sky blue?, 2. How do flowers grow?,
3. I see a rocket in the sky!, 4. Look at the colorful bird!,
5. When will the sun shine?

page 69
1. may 23 2012; May 23, 2012, 2. january 1 2014;
January 1, 2014, 3. june 30 2008; June 30, 2008,
4. october 31 2013; October 31, 2013, 5. Answers
will vary.

Answer Key
Core Skills Language Arts, Grade 1

page 70
1. I can run, jump, and skip., 2. The zoo has lions, bears, zebras, and monkeys., 3. Cars, trucks, and buses drive on the road., 4. Ana, Emma, and Maria play the game., 5. Frank packed pants, shirts, and socks.

page 71
1. friend, 2. skipping, 3. field, 4. hurries

page 72
1. bike, 2. bone, 3. slide, 4. rake, 5. rope, 6. snake

page 73
1. sun, 2. slide, 3. mat, 4. rug

page 74
1. home, 2. road, 3. catch, 4. big

page 75
1. sound, noise, 2. begin, starts, 3. look, see, 4. glad, happy, 5. little, small

page 76
1. down, 2. hard, 3. light, 4. off, 5. in, 6. opened, 7. awake

page 77
1. big, 2. in, 3. new, 4. off, 5. down, 6. soft

page 78
1. know, no, 2. hi, high, 3. eight, ate, 4. flour, flower, 5. sea, see, 6. sale, sail, 7. read, red, 8. hear, here

page 79
1. to, 2. two, 3. to, 4. two, 5. to, 6. two, 7. to, 8. two

page 80
1. a, 2. b, 3. a, 4. b, 5. a, 6. b, 7. b, 8. a

page 81
1. peek, 2. stomped, 3. gigantic, 4. runs, 5. thrilled

page 82
1. not fair, 2. wash again, 3. lock again, 4. not clear, 5. write again

page 83
1. full of care, 2. without clouds, 3. full of hope, 4. without fear, 5. full of cheer

page 84
1. talk, 2. bring, 3. run, 4. give, 5. pass

page 85
1. big meal, 2. huge, 3. crawled, 4. wrote, 5. heavy rainfall

page 86
First, Next, Then, Last

page 87
Answers may vary. 1. backyard, 2. treehouse, 3. birdhouse, 4. sandbox.

page 88
Answers may vary. 1. The birds fly., 2. That frog hops., 3. The fish swims., 4. My dog digs.

page 89
Answers may vary. 1. store, 2. seeds, 3. garden, 4. rain, 5. sun, 6. flowers

page 90
Answers may vary. 1. run, 2. jump, 3. eat, 4. chase, 5. bark, 6. climbs

page 91
Answers will vary. Possible responses are given. 1. cold, 2. crunchy, 3. three, 4. brown, 5. black, 6. white, soft

page 92
Answers will vary. Be sure each written response answers the question.

page 93
Answers will vary.

page 94
Answers will vary.

page 95
I like to dive.

page 97
Harris Park

page 99
Answers will vary. Possible responses: small, dark, pretty, fast

page 101
Danny

page 103
play hide-and-seek

page 105
Birthday Cookies

page 107
1. a b c, 2. f g h, 3. c d e, 4. n o p, 5. h i j, 6. x y z

page 108
1. bird can dig, 2. find give help, 3. name one red, 4. she they we

page 109
1. 2, 3, 1; He likes me., 2. 1, 3, 2; Dave is playing., 3. 3, 1, 2; Anna goes outside., 4. 3, 1, 2; Cat finds Mouse.

page 110
1. All About Dogs, 2. Minnie Fleas, 3. Barker Books

page 111
1. 8, 2. 12, 3. 4, 4. 14

page 112
1, 3, 4, 2

page 113
1. whale, 2. rabbit, 3. monkey, 4. bird

page 114

swim, fly; Drawings will vary.

page 115

Clothing: socks, jacket, shirt, pants; **Food:** apple, pizza, cupcake, carrot

page 116

1. boots, **2.** banana, **3.** tiger, **4.** lake, **5.** baseball, **6.** ice cream

page 117

Answers will vary. Possible responses: Alike: They are both tall. Different: They are made of different things.

page 118

What happened first? Matt was sad because he couldn't find his friends on his birthday.; What happened next? He went for a walk. OR He looked at the plants. OR He saw the plants move.; What happened at the end? His friends had a surprise birthday party for him.